Smith

FLAVOURED
BREADS

FLAVOURED
BREADS

LINDA COLLISTER
Photography by
Patrice de Villiers

RYLAND
PETERS
& SMALL

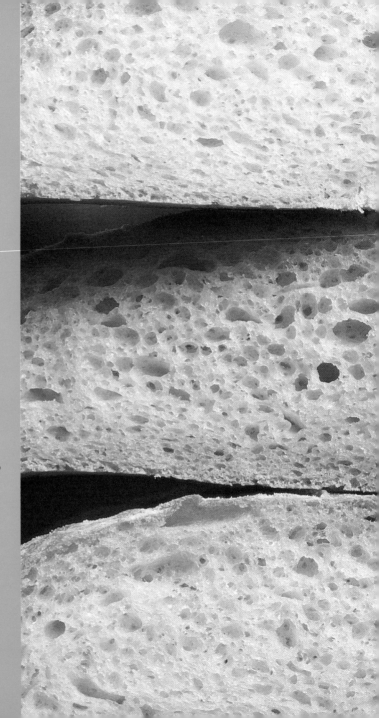

Art Director **Jacqui Small**

Art Editor **Penny Stock**

Editor **Elsa Petersen-Schepelern**

Photography **Patrice de Villiers**

Food Stylist **Linda Collister**

Stylist **Hannah Attwell**

Production **Kate Mackillop**

To Stevie

Notes: Ovens should be preheated to the specified
temperatures – if using a fan-assisted oven, adjust time and
temperature according to the manufacturer's instructions.

Most of the breads in this book can be frozen for up to
1 month. The exceptions are Bacon and Walnut Fougasses
(page 12), Cherry Tomato Focaccia with Basil (page 16),
Rye and Caraway Loaf (page 29) and Multi-seed Bread
(page 35), which should not be frozen.

First Published in Great Britain in 1997
by Ryland Peters & Small
Cavendish House, 51–55 Mortimer Street, London W1N 7TD

Text © Linda Collister 1997
Design and photographs © Ryland Peters & Small 1997
Reprinted in 1998

Printed and bound in Hong Kong

ISBN 1 900518 41 4

A CIP record for this book is available from the British Library

CONTENTS

flavoured
breads

With such exotic, ever-changing variety on the supermarket shelves, why make bread? It saves money, of course, and has a taste and texture worlds away from even the best you can buy. You need no special talent – just flour, yeast, salt, water, a baking sheet, an oven and time.

Much of the flavour in home-made bread comes from quality flours. Top row from left is **spelt**, higher in protein with a greater concentration of vitamins and minerals than ordinary flours.

Malted brown flour makes a light, textured loaf with nutty pieces of wheat. **Strong white bread flour** can be mixed with other flours, such as rye, to lighten them.

Bottom from left, is **coarse stoneground whole-wheat flour**, which makes a chewy, rough-textured loaf. **Stoneground rye flour** used to be a staple in Eastern and Central Europe, but is now usually mixed with wheat flour, or added to sourdoughs for extra flavour.

Rising agents used in breads include (top right) easy-blend dried yeast and fresh yeast (below right). Wrapped in plastic, fresh yeast can be refrigerated for a week or frozen for a month. When you make bread, dried yeast is mixed with flour: fresh yeast with liquid, usually water.

The flavour of dough comes from basic flours (for example, below from left, plain white or wholemeal flour), or from additions such as poppy seeds, rye flour or walnuts.

The quantity of **liquid** needed to form the dough depends on the condition of the flours, the type of flavourings, and even the weather. The ideal texture is soft but not sticky – add extra flour or water to achieve that consistency.

Salt is also crucial. If too little, the dough will rise too fast, then collapse: too much will inhibit or even kill the yeast.

Thorough **kneading** is vital. It develops gluten, the substance in the flour that acts as scaffolding supporting the bubbles of carbon dioxide from the yeast. It also ensures that the yeast is evenly distributed through the dough so it rises uniformly. You can knead by hand, or in a mixer fitted with a dough hook, but not in a food processor.

When dough is left to rise uncovered, it forms a dry crust, and this can result in hard lumps in the baked loaf. So always cover your rising dough with a damp tea towel or a large polythene bag.

Too little **rising time** produces a heavy, small

loaf. Too much is even worse: dough seriously distended by too long or too quick a rise will collapse in the oven.

Preheating the oven is important and requires care. A hot oven kills yeast quickly and prevents over-rising. Every oven has its own personality, so check shelf positions in your handbook and take my cooking times as guidelines, particularly with fan ovens. To test whether a loaf is cooked, unmould it and knock on the bottom with your knuckles: it should sound hollow. If it doesn't, replace and bake it for five more minutes before testing again.

Baked bread should be removed from the sheet or tin and **cooled** on a wire rack; this helps form a good crust. For the best results, **slice** bread only when it's completely cool. Invest in **high quality** loaf tins and baking sheets. They won't warp or scorch in a hot oven, they clean up well without rusting and last a lifetime as well.

bacon and walnut
fougasses

1 tablespoon olive or vegetable oil

85 g rindless bacon, finely diced

60 g walnut pieces,
roughly chopped

700 g unbleached
white bread flour

2 teaspoons sea salt

15 g fresh yeast, crumbled*

300 ml lukewarm water

1 medium egg, beaten

3 tablespoons olive oil

extra flour, for dusting

extra oil, for brushing

several baking sheets, greased

Makes 8 pieces

*To use easy-blend dried yeast,
add one 7 g sachet to the flour,
when you add the salt.*

Heat the oil in a pan, add the bacon and fry until golden and crisp, but not hard. Drain on kitchen paper, then combine well with the walnuts.

Put the flour and salt in a large bowl, mix well, then make a well in the centre. In a small bowl, cream the yeast to a smooth liquid with the water. Tip into the well, then mix in the egg and olive oil.

Gradually work in the flour to make a soft but not sticky dough. If there are crumbs in the bottom of the bowl, add water, 1 tablespoon at a time, until the dough comes together. If the dough sticks to your fingers, work in more flour, about 1 tablespoon at a time.

Turn out the dough on to a lightly floured work surface and knead thoroughly for 10 minutes until the dough feels smooth, very elastic and silky.

Place in a lightly oiled bowl and turn it over so the entire surface is lightly coated with oil.

Cover with a damp tea towel and let rise at room temperature until doubled in size – about 1½ hours. Knock back the dough, then turn out on to a lightly floured surface. Knead in the bacon and nuts until evenly distributed.

Weigh the dough and divide into 8 equal parts. Using a rolling pin, roll each piece into an oval about 21 x 12 x 1 cm. With a sharp knife, cut about 8 slits in a herringbone pattern in each oval. Arrange them, spaced well apart, on the baking sheets.

Lightly cover the baking sheets with a damp tea towel and let rise at cool to normal room temperature until doubled in size – about 45 minutes.

Uncover, lightly brush with oil, then bake in a preheated oven at 200°C (400°F) Gas 6 for about 15–20 minutes until golden brown. Cool on a wire rack.

Variation

Salami Fougasses

Omit the bacon and walnuts. Skin a 100 g piece of *saucisson sec* or salami, dice finely and add after the first rising. Proceed as in the main recipe.

These **attractive**, *oval, individual loaves come from Provence where, these days, they are made* **plain** *or* **flavoured** *with olives, herbs, charcuterie or even candied fruit. Use top-quality bacon – poitrine fumée or dry-cured, thick-cut smoked streaky.*

*This dough is risen **three** times. For an open, light **texture**, don't overload with olive oil.*

focaccia
with rosemary and sea salt

15 g fresh yeast, crumbled*

280 ml water (room temperature)

6–7 tablespoons
extra-virgin olive oil

2 teaspoons sea salt

2 tablespoons finely chopped
fresh rosemary, plus extra sprigs

about 500 g unbleached
white bread flour

2 teaspoons coarse sea salt

extra flour, for dusting

extra oil, for greasing bowl

a roasting or baking tin,
about 25 × 35 cm, greased

Makes 1 loaf

*To use easy-blend dried yeast,
add one 7 g sachet with the
chopped rosemary. Put all the
liquid into the bowl at once and
proceed with the recipe.*

In a small bowl, cream the yeast to a smooth liquid with half the water. Add 3 tablespoons oil and the remaining water. Add the salt, chopped rosemary and half the flour. Beat into the liquid with your hand. When combined, work in enough of the remaining flour to make a soft but not sticky dough. On a lightly floured surface, knead for 10 minutes until very smooth and silky (or for up to 5 minutes at low speed in a mixer fitted with a dough hook). Put into a lightly oiled mixing bowl, turning it over so the entire surface is coated with oil. Cover with a damp tea towel and let rise at cool to normal room temperature until doubled in size – about 2 hours. Knock back the dough, turn out, then shape into a rectangle. Press into the base of the tin, pushing into the corners and patting out to make an even layer. Cover and let rise as before until almost doubled in height – 45 minutes to 1 hour. Flour your fingertips and press into the risen dough to make dimples 1 cm deep. Cover and let rise again until doubled in height – about 1 hour. Press sprigs of rosemary into the dimples and fill with olive oil. Sprinkle with sea salt. Bake in a preheated oven at 220°C (425°F) Gas 7 for 20–25 minutes until golden brown. Cool on a wire rack.

focaccia with pancetta

additional ingredients:

**100–150 g pancetta
or streaky bacon**

**about 3 tablespoons
extra-virgin olive oil**

**sea salt and coarsely
ground black pepper**

a roasting or baking tin,
about 25 × 35 cm, greased

Makes 1 loaf

Follow the recipe on the previous page, omitting the rosemary and sea salt.

During the first rising, grill the pancetta or bacon, discarding any rind and small pieces of bone. Drain and cool on kitchen paper, then chop finely and sprinkle with coarsely ground black pepper.

Knock back the risen dough and knead in the pancetta or bacon. Roll out the dough to fit the tin, then proceed as in the main recipe, drizzling with olive oil to fill the dimples and sprinkling with sea salt and coarsely ground black pepper. Bake, then cool, as in the main recipe.

cherry tomato
focaccia with basil

additional ingredients:

150 g ripe fresh cherry tomatoes

a large bunch of fresh basil

4 tablespoons extra-virgin olive oil

sea salt and black pepper

a roasting or baking tin,
about 25 × 35 cm, greased

Makes 1 loaf

Follow the recipe on the previous page, omitting the fresh rosemary and sea salt.

Cut the tomatoes in half and strip the leaves from a large bunch of fresh basil. Just after making the dimples, push a basil leaf into each hollow, then half a tomato, cut side up. Cover the dough and let rise as before until doubled in height – about 1 hour.

Drizzle with olive oil to moisten the tomatoes and sprinkle with salt and pepper. Bake, then cool, as in the main recipe.

*Two **variations** on the main focaccia recipe.*

*The longer the olives **marinate** in the flavoured oil, the better. For a **sharper** taste, use green olives.*

italian ciabatta
with olives and thyme

Put the olives in a bowl with the olive oil, lemon peel and thyme. Cover and let marinate for 3–4 hours or overnight. Put 500 g flour in a large bowl and make a well in the centre. In a small bowl, cream the yeast to a smooth liquid with 100 ml water, pour into the well, then add the remaining water. Mix to a sticky dough, almost like batter. Cover with a damp tea towel and let rise at normal room temperature for 3–4 hours. It should grow to about 3 times its original size. Check occasionally to make sure the dough has not stuck to the tea towel. Knock back the risen dough. Strain the olives, discard the lemon peel and reserve the oil. Mix the oil and salt into the dough, then gradually work in the remaining flour to make a soft, sticky dough. Cut in half and put 1 portion into another bowl. Mix half the olives into each. Cover with damp tea towels and let rise as before until doubled in size – about 1 hour.

Tip on to a baking sheet. Shape into 2 rectangles, 2.5 cm thick. Push the olives back into the dough, sprinkle with flour and let rise uncovered at room temperature until doubled in size – about 1 hour. Bake in a preheated oven at 220°C (425°F) Gas 7 for 30 minutes until the loaves are brown and sound hollow when tapped underneath. Cool on a wire rack.

150 g black olives, preferably kalamata, pitted

150 ml virgin olive oil

a strip of fresh lemon peel

3 teaspoons chopped fresh thyme

700 g unbleached white bread flour

35 g fresh yeast, crumbled*

450 ml water from the cold tap

2½ teaspoons sea salt

extra flour, for sprinkling

2 baking sheets, well greased

Makes 2 loaves

This recipe is not successful when made with dried yeast.

For this **open-textured** *loaf, use well-flavoured olive oil and good quality, stoneground, organic flour.*

olive oil bread

1 kg unbleached white bread flour

3½ teaspoons sea salt

20 g fresh yeast, crumbled*

about 600 ml water,
at room temperature

100 ml extra-virgin olive oil

extra flour, for dusting

a large baking sheet,
lightly greased

Makes 1 large loaf

*To use easy-blend dried yeast,
add 10 g (1½ × 7 g sachets) to the
flour with the salt, then proceed
with the recipe.*

Combine the flour and salt in a large mixing bowl and make a well in the centre.

In a small bowl, cream the yeast to a smooth liquid with 3 tablespoons of the water. Pour into the well in the flour, adding most of the remaining water. Quickly mix the flour into the liquid, then pour in the oil and continue mixing until the dough comes together. Gradually add the rest of the water if necessary – the dough should be fairly soft, but should hold its shape and not stick to your fingers.

Turn out on to a lightly floured work surface. Knead thoroughly for 10 minutes until the dough is elastic and silky smooth. Place in a large bowl, cover with a damp tea towel and let rise at cool to normal room temperature until doubled in size – about 2 hours.

Turn out on to a floured surface. Do not knock down or knead, but gently shape the dough into a 55 cm-long sausage. Join the ends to make a ring. Transfer to the prepared baking sheet, cover with a damp tea towel, and let rise as before until almost doubled in size – about 1 hour.

Uncover the loaf, dust with flour and bake in a preheated oven at 230°C (450°F) Gas 8 for 10 minutes. Reduce to 190°C (375°F) Gas 5 and bake for another 20 minutes or until it sounds hollow when tapped underneath. Cool on a wire rack.

SPICES AND **SEEDS**

saffron plait

1 heaped teaspoon
saffron strands

150 ml warm water

700 g strong white bread flour

3 teaspoons sea salt

1 teaspoon golden caster sugar

25 g unsalted butter,
chilled and diced

15 g fresh yeast, crumbled*

300 ml skimmed milk,
at room temperature

1 medium egg, beaten

extra flour, for dusting

1 egg beaten with a
good pinch of salt, to glaze

a large baking sheet, greased

Makes 1 large loaf

*To use easy-blend dried yeast,
add one 7 g sachet to the flour
with the salt and sugar, then
proceed with the recipe.*

Toast the saffron on a plate in the oven at 180°C (350°F) Gas 4, without burning, for 10–15 minutes, then crumble into a bowl. Add the warm water, stir, cover and let soak overnight.

Next day, combine the flour, salt and sugar in a large mixing bowl. Add the butter and rub in with your fingertips until the mixture looks like breadcrumbs. Make a well in the centre of the mixture, and pour in the bowl of saffron.

In a small bowl, cream the yeast with the milk until smooth. Stir in the egg, then pour into the well. Work the mixture to form a fairly firm, soft dough. If any dry crumbs remain, work in extra milk, 1 tablespoon at a time. If the dough sticks to your fingers, work in extra flour, 1 tablespoon at a time.

Turn out on to a floured surface and knead thoroughly for 10 minutes (or 5 minutes at low speed in a mixer fitted with a doughhook). The dough should be very elastic and silky smooth. Put into a lightly greased bowl and turn it over so the surface is lightly coated with oil. Cover with a damp tea towel and let rise at normal room temperature until doubled in size – about 1½ hours.

Knock back the dough with your knuckles, then turn out on a floured surface. It should be pliable but not soft, and should hold its shape well. If not, knead in a little more flour.

Weigh the dough, divide into 3–4 equal pieces, and plait as described opposite. Cover with a damp tea-towel and let rise at a cool temperature until almost doubled in size – about 1–1½ hours. Don't let it over-rise or become too soft in a warm place or it will spread.

Brush the top with egg glaze, then bake in a preheated oven at 230°C (450°F) Gas 8 for 15 minutes until golden. Reduce to 200°C (440°F) Gas 6 and bake for 20–30 minutes until it sounds hollow when tapped underneath. Cool on a wire rack.

To make a 3-strand plait:

Using your hands, roll 3 pieces of dough into ropes 40 cm long. Place the 3 ropes on the baking sheet, then plait loosely together. Avoid overstretching the dough. Tuck the ends under to give a good shape.

To make a 4-strand plait:

Using your hands, roll 4 pieces of dough into ropes 33 cm long and 2.5 cm thick. Pinch them firmly together at one end, then arrange vertically in front of you, side by side, slightly apart, with the join at the top. Run the far-left strand under the 2 middle ones, then back over the last it went under. Run the far-right strand under the twisted 2 in the middle, then back over the last it went under. Repeat until all the dough is plaited. Pinch the ends together at the bottom. Transfer to a baking sheet, tucking the ends under to give a neat shape.

*Saffron gives a rich gold colour and a deep, **aromatic** flavour to bread dough. The longer the saffron is soaked, the better.*

Made to celebrate the Jewish sabbath, this rich, sweet bread can be flavoured with honey, saffron or spices.

vanilla challah

230 ml skimmed milk

2 tablespoons golden caster sugar

1 vanilla pod, split lengthways

15 g fresh yeast, crumbled*

700 g unbleached
white bread flour

2½ teaspoons sea salt

85 g unsalted butter,
melted and cooled

3 medium eggs, beaten

extra flour, for dusting

vegetable oil, for greasing

1 egg yolk beaten with
a pinch of salt,to glaze

a large baking sheet, greased
Makes 1 loaf

*To use easy-blend dried yeast,
add one 7 g sachet to the flour
with the salt and sugar, then
proceed with the recipe.*

Heat the milk, sugar and vanilla pod in a small pan until just steaming. Cover and set aside while the milk cools to lukewarm. Remove the pod and scrape the seeds into the milk. In a small bowl, cream the yeast and milk to a smooth liquid. Mix the flour and salt in a bowl, make a well in the centre, pour the liquid, butter and eggs into the well, then mix. Work in the flour to make a soft but not sticky dough. If too dry, add tepid water 1 tablespoon at a time. If sticky and soft, work in flour 1 tablespoon at a time. Turn out on a floured surface and knead for 10 minutes until silky and elastic. Return to the washed and greased bowl and turn until the surface is lightly coated with oil. Cover with a damp tea towel and let rise in a cool spot until doubled in size – 1½–2 hours. Knock back the dough, cover and let rise as before – about 45 minutes. Knock back again and knead in the bowl for 1 minute. Let rest in the bowl, covered with the tea towel, for 5 minutes. Cover loosely with a damp tea towel and let rise as before until doubled in size – about 45 minutes.

Divide and plait the dough as described in the previous recipe. Brush with 2 thin coats of egg-yolk glaze and bake in a preheated oven at 220°C (425°F) Gas 7 for 10 minutes. Glaze again and reduce the heat to 190°C (375°F) Gas 5 and bake for 30 minutes or until the loaf is golden brown and sounds hollow when tapped underneath. Cool on a wire rack.

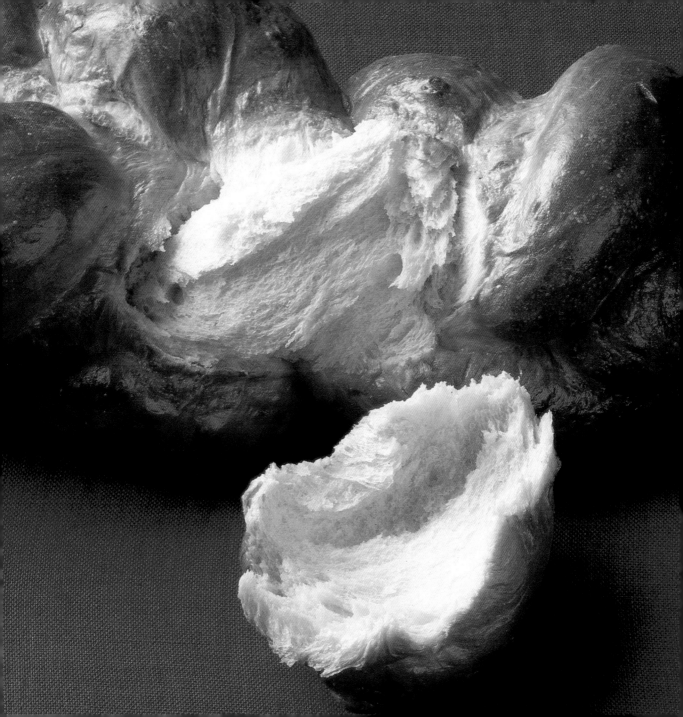

A loaf with the **distinctive** *taste of rye without the heavy texture — stoneground rye flour will produce the best flavour.*

rye and caraway loaf

Mix the two flours, caraway seeds and salt in a large bowl and make a well in the centre.

In a small bowl, cream the yeast to a smooth liquid with a little of the water. Pour into the well with the rest of the water, then mix in the flour to make a soft but not sticky dough. If too sticky, add white flour, 1 tablespoon at a time. If there are dry crumbs in the bottom of the bowl and the dough is stiff and hard to work, add extra water, 1 tablespoon at a time. Turn out on to a lightly floured surface and knead thoroughly for 10 minutes. Return to the bowl, cover with a damp tea towel and let rise until doubled in size — about 2 hours. Knock back the dough with your knuckles, then turn out on to a lightly floured surface. Knead lightly into an oval. With the edge of your hand, make a crease down the middle, then roll the dough over to make a sausage. Put the seam underneath so the top is smooth and evenly shaped. Place on the baking sheet, cover and let rise until doubled in size — about 1 hour.

Uncover the loaf and slash the top several times with a very sharp knife. Bake in a preheated oven at 200°C (400°F) Gas 6 for 15 minutes until golden, then reduce to 190°C (375°F) Gas 5 and bake for a further 20–25 minutes until the loaf sounds hollow when tapped underneath. Cool on a wire rack.

400 g unbleached white bread flour

300 g rye flour

2 tablespoons caraway seeds

3 teaspoons sea salt

15 g fresh yeast, crumbled*

450 ml cold water

extra flour, for dusting

a baking sheet, greased

Makes 1 large loaf

To use easy-blend dried yeast, mix one 7 g sachet with the flours, seeds, and salt. Add the water and proceed with the recipe.

*A mixed-flour loaf, **speckled** with dried chilli flakes. Wonderful with smoked salmon and cream cheese – the combination of hot, cold and savoury is irresistible.*

chilli pepper bread

2–3 teaspoons dried chilli flakes (the quantity depends on their strength and your courage)

250 g strong white bread flour

250 g stoneground wholemeal bread flour

250 g stoneground rye flour

3 teaspoons sea salt

15 g fresh yeast, crumbled*

450 ml water, at room temperature

extra flour, for dusting

one 1 kg loaf tin, greased

Makes 1 large loaf

*To use dried easy-blend yeast, mix one 7 g sachet with the chilli flakes, flours and salt. Add all the liquid at once, and proceed with the recipe.

Mix the chilli, flours and salt in a large bowl. In a small bowl, cream the yeast to a smooth paste with a little of the water. Make a well in the flour mixture, pour in the yeast paste and the rest of the water. Gradually work the flour into the liquid to make a soft but not sticky dough. If it sticks to your hands, add a little more white flour. If there are dry crumbs in the bowl and the dough is stiff and hard to work, add water, about 1 tablespoon at a time. Turn out on to a lightly floured surface and knead for 10 minutes until very elastic and pliable. Return to the bowl, cover with a damp tea towel and let rise at cool to normal room temperature until doubled in size – about 2 hours.

Knock back the risen dough with your knuckles, then turn out on to a lightly floured surface and shape to fit your tin. Put it in the tin and tuck under the ends to make a neat shape (the top of the dough should be halfway up the sides of the tin). Cover and leave at cool to normal room temperature until the dough rises just above the rim of the tin – about 1½ hours. Bake in a preheated oven at 230°C (450°F) Gas 8 for about 15 minutes. Reduce to 200°C (400°F) Gas 6 and cook for 25–30 minutes until the loaf sounds hollow when removed from the tin and tapped underneath. Cool on a wire rack.

*A **speckled**, airy bread – great with soups and sandwiches.*
poppy seed loaf

40 g poppy seeds

650 g unbleached white bread flour

2 teaspoons sea salt

50 g unsalted butter, chilled and diced

1½ tablespoons golden caster sugar

15 g fresh yeast, crumbled*

375 ml skimmed milk, at room temperature

1 medium egg, beaten

extra flour, for dusting

extra milk, for brushing

one 900 g loaf tin, greased

Makes 1 large loaf

To use easy-blend dried yeast, add one 7 g sachet to the flour with the salt and poppy seeds, then proceed with the recipe.

Mix the seeds, flour and salt in a large bowl. Add the butter and rub in with your fingertips until the mixture resembles fine crumbs. Stir in the sugar and make a well in the centre. In a small bowl, cream the yeast to a smooth liquid with a little of the milk. Pour into the well with the egg and remaining milk.

Work the flour into the liquid to make a soft but not sticky dough. Turn out on to a lightly floured surface and knead thoroughly for 10 minutes. Return to the bowl, cover with a damp tea towel and let rise at cool to normal room temperature until doubled in size – about 1½–2 hours.

Knock back the risen dough, then turn out on to a lightly floured surface. Knead it smooth for 1 minute, then pat into a rectangle the length of the tin and about 1 cm thick. Roll up the dough like a Swiss roll from one short end. Pinch the seam with your fingers to seal, then put the dough into the tin, seam side down, tucking the ends underneath. The tin should be half filled. Cover with a damp tea towel and let rise at room temperature until doubled in size – about 1 hour.

Uncover and brush with milk. Bake in a preheated oven at 230°C (450°F) Gas 8 for 15 minutes, reduce to 200°C (400°F) Gas 6 and bake for 20–30 minutes, until the turned-out loaf sounds hollow when tapped underneath. Cool on a wire rack.

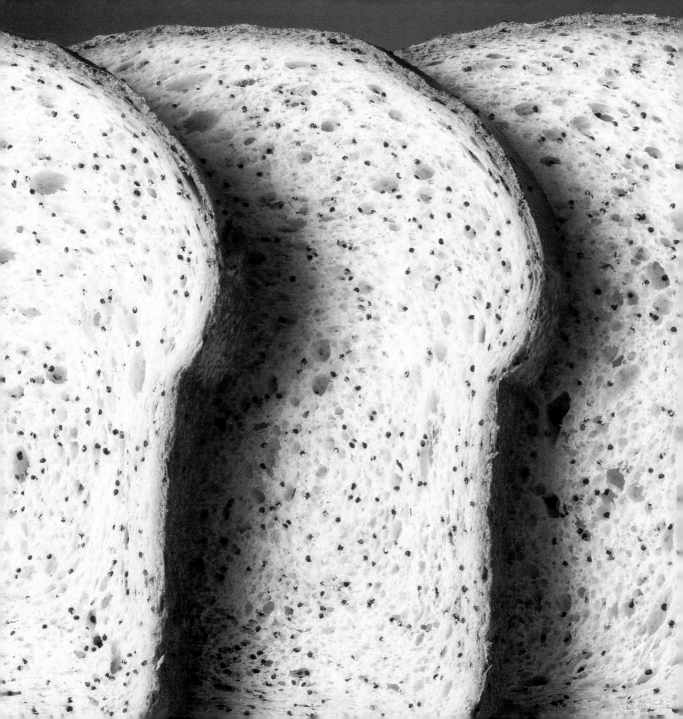

multi-seed bread

Put the flours, seeds (except the garnish) and salt in a large bowl and mix thoroughly. Make a well in the centre. In a small bowl, cream the yeast to a smooth liquid with a little of the water. Pour into the well, then add the oil and all but 50 ml of the water. Gradually work the flour mixture into the liquid to make a soft but not sticky dough, adding more water as necessary. Turn out on to a lightly floured work surface and knead thoroughly for about 10 minutes. Return the dough to the bowl, cover with a damp tea towel, and let rise at cool to normal room temperature until doubled in size – about 1½–2 hours.

Knock back the dough with your knuckles, turn out of the bowl on to a lightly floured surface, knead for 1 minute, then divide in half. Shape each half to fit a loaf tin, then put into the tins, tucking the ends under – the dough should half-fill each tin. Cover and let rise until doubled in size – about 1 hour. Using a sharp knife, slash the top of each loaf several times. Brush both with milk, then sprinkle with the extra seeds. Bake in a preheated oven at 200°C (400°F) Gas 6 for about 35 minutes until the loaves are golden and sound hollow when turned out and tapped underneath. Cool on a wire rack.

Crammed full of seeds and with plenty of texture and *flavour*, this dense loaf makes great toast.

450 g unbleached white bread flour

200 g spelt flour

20 g poppy seeds

30 g linseeds

30 g sesame seeds

30 g sunflower seeds

30 g pumpkin seeds

3 teaspoons sea salt

15 g fresh yeast, crumbled*

425–450 ml water, at room temperature

1 tablespoon olive oil

extra flour, for dusting

milk, for brushing

extra linseeds and sesame seeds, to finish

two 450 g loaf tins, greased

Makes 2 medium loaves

*To use easy-blend dried yeast, mix one 7 g sachet with the flours, add the water, then proceed with the recipe.

molasses mixed grain
pumpernickel

250 g stoneground rye flour

150 g coarse wholemeal bread flour

100 g spelt flour

50 g barley flour

50 g fine oatmeal

50 g buckwheat flour

100 g white bread flour

2 teaspoons sea salt

1½ tablespoons
dark muscovado sugar

20 g fresh yeast, crumbled*

370 ml water

50 g molasses

1 tablespoon vegetable oil

one 900 g loaf tin, greased

Makes 1 large loaf

*To use easy-blend dried yeast,
mix 10 g (1½ sachets) with the
white flour. Put other flours, salt
and sugar in a bowl, make a well,
add the water. Stir in the yeast and
proceed with the recipe.*

Mix the flours, oatmeal, salt and sugar in a large mixing bowl, and make a well in the centre.

In a small bowl, cream the yeast to a smooth liquid together with a little of the water. Stir in the rest of the water, then tip it into the well.

Mix some of the flour into the liquid to make a thick, smooth batter in the well. Sprinkle a little flour over the batter to prevent a skin forming, then cover and leave the bowl for 30 minutes until the batter looks bubbly.

Stir the molasses and oil into the batter, then gradually work in the rest of the flour to make a soft, slightly sticky dough. It will seem heavier and more difficult to work than other bread doughs, but if it is dry or too hard to work, you may need to add a little extra water. If it seems wet or too sticky, add a little extra white flour, 1 tablespoon at a time.

Turn out on to a floured surface and knead thoroughly for about 5 minutes. Cover the dough with an upturned bowl, let rest for about 5 minutes, then knead for a further 5 minutes. Return the dough to the bowl, cover with a damp tea towel and let rise at normal room temperature until doubled in size – about 3 hours .

Knock back the risen dough, then turn out on to a lightly floured work surface and knead for 1 minute. Shape into a loaf to fit the tin, then put in the dough, pushing it into the corners – the top of the dough should be halfway up the tin.

Cover with a damp tea towel and let rise at normal room temperature until the dough reaches the top of the loaf tin – about 1½–2 hours.

Bake in a preheated oven at 200°C (400°F) Gas 6 for about 40 minutes or until the loaf is dark brown and sounds hollow when removed from the tin and tapped underneath.

Cool completely on a wire rack, then keep wrapped in greaseproof paper for at least 1–2 days before slicing thinly. This loaf will mature when kept and will taste best about 4 days after baking.

Variation

Raisin Pumpernickel

Place 90 g of raisins or sultanas in a bowl, pour over orange juice to cover and let soak for about 1 hour. Drain, then add the fruit to the dough just before shaping into a loaf. Proceed as in the main recipe.

Molasses produces the traditional dark colour in this dense, rich bread made with a mixture of flours, predominantly rye.

spelt sourdough

10 g fresh yeast, crumbled*

600 ml water at room temperature

550 g spelt flour

3 teaspoons sea salt

about 350 g strong
white bread flour

extra flour, for dusting

a large baking sheet, floured

Makes 1 large loaf

**I have had variable results with
easy-blend yeast and prefer fresh
yeast for this recipe.*

Cream the yeast in a bowl with half the water until smooth. Stir in 300 g spelt flour to make a thick batter, cover with a damp tea towel and set aside for 24 hours until it looks bubbly and slightly grey. Next day, stir in the remaining water to make a smooth batter. Transfer to a larger bowl, beat in the salt and remaining spelt flour with your hand, then gradually work in enough white flour to make a soft but not sticky dough (the amount depends on the quality of the spelt flour). Turn out on to a floured surface and knead for 10 minutes. If it sticks to your fingers, work in extra white flour. Return to the bowl, cover with a damp tea towel and let rise at cool to normal room temperature until doubled in size – about 3 hours. Knock back the dough, turn out on to a floured surface and knead for 1 minute. It should be firm enough to hold its shape during baking: if too soft, work in extra flour.

Shape into a round loaf and place on the baking sheet. Cover loosely and let rise as before until almost doubled in size – 1½–2 hours. Slash the top several times with a sharp knife, sprinkle with white flour, then bake in a preheated oven at 220°C (425°F) Gas 7 for 20 minutes. Reduce to 200°C (400°F) Gas 6 and bake for 15 minutes or until the loaf sounds hollow when tapped underneath. Cool on a wire rack. This bread keeps well: freeze for up to 1 month.

Spelt flour has a _nutty_ flavour and has recently become popular with _organic_ farmers.

coarse wholemeal
beer bread

**400 g stoneground
wholemeal bread flour**

**100 g coarsely ground wholemeal
bread flour or wheaten bread flour**

2 teaspoons sea salt

15 g fresh yeast, crumbled*

1 tablespoon lukewarm water

**about 350 ml beer,
at room temperature**

extra flour, for dusting

a baking sheet, greased

Makes 1 medium loaf

*To use easy-blend dried yeast,
add one 7 g sachet to the flour,
then proceed with the recipe. Omit
the water and add 1 extra
tablespoon of beer.*

Mix the flours and salt in a large bowl. Make a well in the centre. In a small bowl, cream the yeast and water to a smooth paste. Add it and the beer to the well in the flour. Mix to a soft but not sticky dough, working it for several minutes before adding anything else.

The amount of liquid you need will depend on the flour, but the dough will feel very different from a white bread dough. If it seems very wet, add extra flour, 1 tablespoon at a time. If stiff and dry, with dry crumbs in the bottom of the bowl, work in extra beer or water, 1 tablespoon at a time.

Knead for 5–7 minutes on a floured surface until the dough is smooth and pliable. Return to the bowl, cover with a damp cloth, and let rise at normal room temperature until doubled in size – about 2 hours.

Knock back the risen dough and shape into a ball. Place on the baking sheet, cover loosely with a damp tea towel and let rise again as before until doubled in size – about 1 hour. Uncover the loaf, slash the top with a sharp knife, sprinkle with coarse wholemeal flour and bake in a preheated oven at 220°C (425°F) Gas 7 for 30–35 minutes until the loaf is golden brown and sounds hollow when tapped underneath. Cool on a wire rack.

German smoked beer, brown ale or stout give **deepest** *flavour: pale ale a more subtle taste.*

honeynut loaf

350 g stoneground
wholemeal bread flour

350 g unbleached
white bread flour

2½ teaspoons sea salt

20 g fresh yeast, crumbled*

350 ml water at room temperature

3 tablespoons
well-flavoured honey

extra flour, for dusting

300 g nuts (any combination of
walnuts, hazelnuts, almonds,
cashews or macadamias), lightly
toasted and roughly chopped

2 baking sheets, greased

Makes 2 medium loaves

*To use easy-blend yeast powder,
mix one 7 g sachet with the flour
and salt, add the water and honey,
then proceed with the recipe.*

Mix the flours and salt together in a large mixing bowl and make a well in the centre.

In a small bowl, cream the yeast to a smooth liquid with a little of the water, then tip into the well in the flour.

Dissolve the honey in the rest of the water and add it to the well. Gradually work the flour into the liquid to make a soft but not sticky dough.

If the dough sticks to your fingers, work in extra flour, about 1 tablespoon at a time. If there are dry crumbs in the bottom of the bowl – or the dough seems stiff and hard to work – add extra water, 1 tablespoon at a time.

Turn out on to a lightly floured surface and knead thoroughly for 10 minutes until smooth and elastic.

Flatten the dough with your hand, sprinkle about a third of the nuts over the dough, then fold it over and over to mix them. Repeat this process twice, then shape the dough into a ball and return it to the bowl.

Cover with a damp tea towel and let rise at cool to normal room temperature until doubled in size – about 2 hours.

Knock back the risen dough with your knuckles, then turn out on to a floured surface and knead for 1 minute to ensure the nuts are evenly distributed.

Divide the dough in half. Shape each portion into a neat ball, pushing back any nuts that protrude or escape.

Place the balls of dough on a baking sheet, cover as before, and let rise at cool to normal room temperature until doubled

Make this well-flavoured bread, loaded with nuts, with a mixture of flours and a pungent honey, such as heather. Use any combination of nuts, but for the best taste, they should be lightly toasted. Serve with butter, cream cheese or cheese.

in size – about 1½ hours. Uncover the risen loaves and slash the tops diagonally several times with a very sharp knife. Bake in a preheated oven at 220°C (425°F) Gas 7 for about 15 minutes, then reduce the temperature to 190°C (375°F) Gas 5 and bake for a further 20–25 minutes.

The loaves should sound hollow when removed from the baking sheet and tapped underneath. Cool on a wire rack. Eat within 4 days or freeze for up to 1 month.

Variation

New England Maple Nut Loaf

A wonderful combination of traditional American ingredients; dried cranberries, maple syrup and pecan nuts.

Omit the roasted nuts from the main recipe and add 75 g dried cranberries and 150 g pecan nut broken into pieces. Substitute 3 tablespoons maple syrup instead of the honey, and proceed as in the main recipe.

Use a good *sugarless* muesli with ingredients such as raisins, dates, wheat flakes, oat flakes, apples, apricots, hazelnuts, almonds and raisins.

muesli round

Put the flours, muesli and salt into a large bowl and mix well. Make a well in the centre.

In a small bowl, cream the yeast to a smooth liquid with 3 tablespoons of the milk mixture. Stir in the rest of the liquid, the honey and oil, then pour into the well. Gradually mix the dry ingredients into the liquid to make a fairly firm dough. If it seems dry or stiff, or there are dry crumbs in the bottom of the bowl, work in extra milk or water, 1 tablespoon at a time. If the dough sticks to your fingers, knead in extra white flour, 1 tablespoon at a time. The amount of liquid needed will depend on the muesli mix.

Turn out on to a lightly floured surface and knead for about 5 minutes. Place in the bowl, cover with a damp tea towel and leave at room temperature until doubled in size – 1–1½ hours.

Turn out on to a lightly floured surface and knead for 1 minute. Shape into a round loaf 20 cm across. Put on the prepared baking sheet and score into 8 segments with a very sharp knife. Cover and let rise as before – about 1 hour. Uncover and sprinkle with wholemeal flour. Cook in a preheated oven at 220°C (425°F) Gas 7 for 30 minutes, or until it sounds hollow when tapped underneath. Cool on a wire rack.

500 g strong white bread flour

100 g stoneground wholemeal flour

250 g unsweetened muesli

2 teaspoons salt

15 g fresh yeast, crumbled*

about 400 ml milk and water mixed, at room temperature

1 tablespoon honey

2 tablespoons vegetable oil

extra flour, for dusting

a baking sheet, greased

Makes 1 large round loaf

To use easy-blend dried yeast, mix one 7 g sachet with the two kinds of flour, the muesli and salt. Pour in all the liquids, then proceed with the recipe.

49

blue cheese and
walnut twist

300 g unbleached
white bread flour

1 teaspoon sea salt

40 g butter, chilled and diced

10 g fresh yeast, crumbled*

50 ml milk mixed with 50 ml
water, at room temperature

1 medium egg, beaten

extra flour, for dusting

Cream Cheese and Walnut Filling:

200 g cream cheese

1 tablespoon milk

50 g finely ground walnuts

125 g blue cheese

125 g walnut pieces

freshly ground black pepper

a baking sheet, greased

Makes 1 loaf

*To use easy-blend dried yeast,
mix 2 teaspoons with the flour and
salt, then proceed with the recipe.*

Mix the flour and salt in a large bowl. Rub in the butter with your fingertips until the mixture looks like fine crumbs. Make a well in the centre.

In a small bowl, cream the yeast with the milk and water until smooth. Mix in the egg, then pour into the well. Gradually work in the flour to make a soft but not sticky dough.

Turn out on to a floured surface and knead for 10 minutes until smooth, silky and elastic. Return to the bowl, cover with a damp tea towel and let rise at normal room temperature until doubled in size – about 1 hour.

To make the filling, beat the cream cheese and milk until soft, then beat in the walnuts and black pepper. Crumble the blue cheese into small chunks and mix with the walnut pieces.

Knock back the risen dough, then roll out on a lightly floured surface into a rectangle, 33 x 30 cm. Spread with the cheese mixture, then scatter blue cheese and walnuts over the top. Roll up the dough fairly tightly from one long side, like a Swiss roll, then roll this into a longer, thinner cylinder about 60 cm long. Cut in half lengthways with a sharp knife. Twist the halves together, cut sides up, and shape into a neat ring on the baking sheet.

Cover loosely with a damp tea towel and let rise at room temperature until doubled in size – 45 minutes to 1 hour. Bake in a preheated oven at 200°C (400°F) Gas 6 for 25 minutes, or until firm and golden. Cool on a wire rack.

A flavourful loaf, not too sweet – good with cold meat and pickles.
sour cherry loaf

350 g unbleached
white bread flour

150 g rye flour,
stoneground if possible

80 g dried sour cherries

2 teaspoons sea salt

15 g fresh yeast, crumbled*

about 300 ml water
from the cold tap

extra flour, for dusting

a baking sheet, greased

Makes 1 medium loaf

*To use easy-blend dried yeast,
add one 7 g sachet to the flour,
then proceed with the recipe.*

Mix the flours, dried sour cherries and salt in a large bowl and make a well in the centre. In a small bowl, cream the yeast with half the water until smooth. Pour into the well, add the remaining water, then gradually mix in the flour to make a soft but not sticky dough. If it seems sticky and difficult to work, mix in white flour 1 tablespoon at a time. If stiff and dry, with crumbs in the bottom of the bowl, work in water, 1 tablespoon at a time (the amount depends on the quality of the flour). Turn out on to a lightly floured surface and knead for about 10 minutes until satiny and elastic. Return to the bowl, cover with a damp tea towel and let rise at cool to normal room temperature until doubled in size – about 2 hours.

Knock back the dough and turn out on to a lightly floured surface. Gently knead into an oval. With the edge of your hand, make a crease down the middle, then roll the dough over to make a sausage shape about 25 cm long. Place, seam side down, on the baking sheet. Cover and let rise at normal room temperature until doubled in size – about 1 hour. Uncover the loaf and slash several times across the top with a very sharp knife. Bake in a preheated oven at 220°C (425°F) Gas 7 for 15 minutes until golden. Reduce to 190°C (375°F) Gas 5 and bake 10–15 minutes until the loaf sounds hollow when tapped underneath. Cool on a wire rack.

VEGETABLES **AND CHEESE**

Slow-cooked onion and **rye** *flour give* **flavour** *without pungency.*
onion rolls

1 large onion, finely chopped

½ teaspoon caster sugar

25 g unsalted butter

400 g strong white bread flour

100 g rye flour,
preferably stoneground

2½ teaspoons sea salt

15 g fresh yeast, crumbled*

300 ml water, at room temperature

extra flour, for dusting

1 egg, beaten with a pinch
of salt, to glaze

2 baking sheets, greased

Makes 14

*To use easy-blend dried yeast,
mix one 7 g sachet with the flours
and salt, add the water and onion
mixture, then proceed with the
recipe.*

Put the onion, sugar and butter in a heavy pan and cook slowly, stirring, until soft and slightly caramelized. Cool.

Mix the flours and salt in a bowl and make a well in the centre. In a small bowl, cream the yeast with a little water until smooth. Add to the well with the onion and remaining water. Work in the flour to make a soft but not sticky dough.

If it sticks to your fingers or the bowl, work in white flour, 1 tablespoon at a time. If it seems stiff, with dry crumbs in the bowl, slowly work in water, 1 tablespoon at a time.

Turn out on to a floured surface and knead for 10 minutes until very smooth and elastic. Return to the bowl, cover with a damp tea towel and let rise at cool to normal room temperature until doubled in size – about 1–1½ hours.

Knock back the dough, turn out on to a floured surface and knead for 1 minute. Weigh and divide into 14 equal pieces. Shape into balls and place well apart on the baking sheets. To make the onion shapes, pinch the centres, drawing them up to make a stalk. Cover with a damp cloth – to avoid flattening the stalks, use upturned bowls to support the towel. Let rise for 30 minutes, until doubled in size.

Brush with egg glaze, then bake in a preheated oven at 220°C (425°F) Gas 7 for about 15–20 minutes until shiny golden brown. Cool on a wire rack.

garlic knots

Put the flour and salt in a large bowl and make a well in the centre. In a small bowl, cream the yeast with a little water until smooth. Stir in the oil, tip into the well, then work in the flour to make a soft but not sticky dough. If too sticky, work in extra flour, 1 tablespoon at a time. If there are dry crumbs in the bowl, work in extra water a little at a time.

Turn out on to a floured surface and knead for 10 minutes until smooth, silky and elastic. Return to the bowl, cover with a damp tea towel and let rise at cool to normal room temperature until doubled in size – about 1½–2 hours .

Cook the garlic in a preheated oven at 190°C (375°F) Gas 5 for 10 minutes until the skin is split and golden and the flesh soft and ripe smelling. Cool and peel, add salt, then mash the garlic into a rough paste with the back of a knife.

Knock back the risen dough, then weigh. Turn out on to a floured surface and divide into 12 equal pieces. Shape into sausages about 20 cm long and flatten slightly. Spread the garlic paste on the top, then tie into knots. Place well apart on the baking sheets, cover loosely with a damp tea towel, and let rise until doubled in size – about 45 minutes. Brush with the egg glaze, then bake in a preheated oven at 220°C (425°F) Gas 7 for 10–15 minutes golden brown and sound hollow when tapped underneath. Cool on a wire rack.

Roasted garlic produces a delicious *aroma* with no harsh taste.

500 g strong white bread flour

1½ teaspoons sea salt

10 g fresh yeast, crumbled*

300 ml water from the cold tap

1 tablespoon virgin olive oil

12 unpeeled garlic cloves

a pinch of salt

extra flour, for dusting

1 egg, beaten with a pinch of salt, to glaze

2 baking sheets, greased

Makes 12

*To use easy-blend dried yeast, mix 5 g (⅔ of a 7 g sachet) with the flour and salt. Proceed with the recipe.

Pumpkin makes a fine, soft, *golden bread that toasts well.*

pumpkin bread

Peel the pumpkin and remove the seeds. Dice the flesh into 1 cm cubes – you will need 400 g.
Without adding water, cook the cubes in a steamer or microwave until they soften. Put them into a food processor with the oil and purée until smooth. Let cool until just lukewarm, then mix in the salt and sugar.
In a small bowl, cream the yeast to a smooth paste with 1 tablespoon of lukewarm water. Mix the paste into the purée.
Put the flour into a large mixing bowl and make a well in the centre. Spoon the purée into the well, then mix in the flour to make a soft but not sticky dough. Turn out on to a floured work surface and knead thoroughly for 5 minutes (or 3 minutes at low speed in a mixer with a dough hook).
Shape the dough into a round loaf about 18 cm across and put it on the baking sheet. Cover and let rise at normal room temperature until doubled in size – about 1½ hours.
Press your thumb into the middle of the risen loaf to make a small hollow, then carefully brush the loaf with the egg glaze. Score the loaf into segments with a sharp knife, then bake in a preheated oven at 200°C (400°F) Gas 6 for about 30 minutes until it is golden brown and sounds hollow when tapped underneath. Cool on a wire rack.

700 g pumpkin, Japanese kabocha or other winter squash

1 tablespoon virgin olive oil

2½ teaspoons sea salt

2 teaspoons golden caster sugar

15 g fresh yeast, crumbled*

350 g strong white bread flour

extra flour, for dusting

1 egg, beaten with a pinch of salt, to glaze

a baking sheet, greased

Makes 1 medium loaf

To use easy-blend dried yeast, mix one 7 g sachet with the flour, then work in the pumpkin purée. If the dough seems dry or there are dry crumbs in the bottom of the bowl, work in a little cold water.

easy cheese brioche

15 g fresh yeast*

100 ml lukewarm skimmed milk

2 medium eggs

1 teaspoon sea salt

¼ teaspoon cayenne pepper

300 g strong white bread flour

50 g unsalted butter, softened

100 g Gruyère cheese, grated,
plus 25 g extra, to finish

extra flour, for dusting

1 egg, beaten with a large pinch
of salt, to glaze

one 500 g loaf tin, greased

Makes 1 medium loaf

*To use easy-blend dried yeast,
mix one 7 g sachet with the flour
and work into the liquids in the
bowl. Proceed with the recipe.*

Crumble the yeast into the bowl of a free-standing mixer. Pour in the milk and mix with the whisk attachment. Whisk in the eggs, then the salt and cayenne pepper.

Using the dough hook at low speed, gradually work in the flour to make a soft but not sticky dough. Knead in the machine at low speed for another 5 minutes until smooth and elastic.

Add the softened butter and knead for another 3–4 minutes until completely incorporated. Cover and let rise at normal room temperature until doubled in size – about 1½ hours.

Knead the grated cheese into the dough for about 1 minute at slow speed, then turn out on to a floured surface and shape into a loaf to fit the tin.

Put in the tin, then cover with a damp cloth and leave at normal room temperature until doubled in size – about 1 hour (the dough should just reach the rim of the tin).

Gently brush the risen loaf with egg glaze, taking care not to glue it to the sides of the tin.

Sprinkle with the extra cheese and bake in a preheated oven at 200°C (400°F) Gas 6 for about 35 minutes until it turns golden brown and sounds hollow when turned out and tapped underneath. Cool on a wire rack.

A rich, light, *tangy* loaf – and *easily* made in a mixer, unlike a classic brioche. Serve it with cheese, salad or soup.

cheese baps
with cheddar and onion

650 g unbleached white bread flour

2 teaspoons sea salt

1 teaspoon powdered mustard

150 g cheddar cheese, grated

40 g spring onions, finely chopped

15 g fresh yeast, crumbled*

200 ml skimmed milk,
at room temperature

200 ml water, at room temperature

extra flour, for dusting

oil, for greasing bowl

milk, for glazing

50 g mature cheddar cheese,
for sprinkling

2 baking sheets, lightly greased

Makes 12

*To use easy-blend dried yeast,
add one 7 g sachet to the flour,
then proceed with the recipe.*

Mix the flour, salt, mustard, cheese and onions in a large bowl. Make a well in the centre.

In a small bowl, cream the yeast to a smooth liquid with the milk, then stir in the water. Pour into the well in the flour. Gradually work the flour into the liquid to make a soft but not sticky dough.

Turn out on to a floured surface and knead for 10 minutes until it feels smooth and elastic. It can also be kneaded for 5 minutes at low speed in a mixer fitted with a dough hook. Put the dough into a lightly greased bowl, turning it so the entire surface is lightly coated with oil. Cover with a damp tea towel and let rise until doubled in size – about 1½–2 hours. Knock back the dough, then turn out on to a floured surface and knead for a few seconds. Divide into 12 and pat into ovals about 11 x 8 x 3 cm. Arrange well apart on the baking sheets. Brush with milk, then sprinkle with cheese. Let rise until doubled in size – about 30 minutes.

Press your thumb into the middle of each bap, then bake in a preheated oven at 220°C (425°F) Gas 7 for 15 minutes until golden. Cool on a wire rack.

For the best flavour, use *mature* cheese: much so-called cheddar is too bland for this recipe.